SCHOOL SECRETARIES

Cindy Klingel and Robert B. Noyed

The Rourke Press, Inc.
Vero Beach, Florida 32964

PHOTO CREDITS
© Flanagan Publishing Services/Romie Flanagan

We would like to thank the students and staff of Channing Memorial
School for their valuable assistance in producing this book.

Library of Congress Cataloging-in-Publication Data

Klingel, Cynthia Fitterer
    School secretaries / Cindy Klingel, Robert B. Noyed.
        p. cm. — (My school helpers)
    Includes index.
    Summary: Describes the school secretary's day as she works with students,
parents, teachers, and other school workers.
    ISBN 1-57103-328-9
    1. School secretaries—Juvenile literature. [1. School secretaries.
2. Occupations.] I. Noyed, Robert B. II. Title.

LB2844.4 .K45 2001
371.2'—dc21   99-088932
                                                               CIP

Printed in the USA

CONTENTS

About the Authors

Cindy Klingel has worked as a high school English teacher and an elementary teacher. She is currently the curriculum director for a Minnesota school district. Writing children's books is another way that continues her passion for sharing the written word with children. Cindy Klingel is a frequent visitor to the children's section of bookstores and enjoys spending time with her many friends, family, and two daughters.

Bob Noyed started his career as a newspaper reporter. Since then, he has worked in communications and public relations for more than fourteen years for a Minnesota school district. He enjoys writing books for children and finds that it brings a different feeling of challenge and accomplishment from other writing projects. He is an avid reader who also enjoys music, theater, travelling, and spending time with his wife, son, and daughter.

The person you know best at school is probably your teacher. But many other school helpers keep the school running. You may not know about all they do. Here are some of the many things your school secretary does.

The secretary arrives at school. She is one of the first people there. Soon, the phone will be ringing and students and teachers will be coming into the office. She is ready for another busy day!

The school secretary's day starts early.

The school secretary is responsible for many things. She is a helper for everyone. Parents, students, teachers, and other people who work in the school **rely on** her.

The secretary's office is a center of information at the school.

Parents ask the school secretary for information. They drop off items to be delivered to students. The school secretary answers many phone calls from parents. They give her important information about the students. They may ask questions about special events happening at the school.

School secretaries answer many questions.

Students need the school secretary, too. They may come to the office before, during, and after school with questions for her. When students are ill, sometimes it is the school secretary who helps them.

Students often need the school secretary to help them.

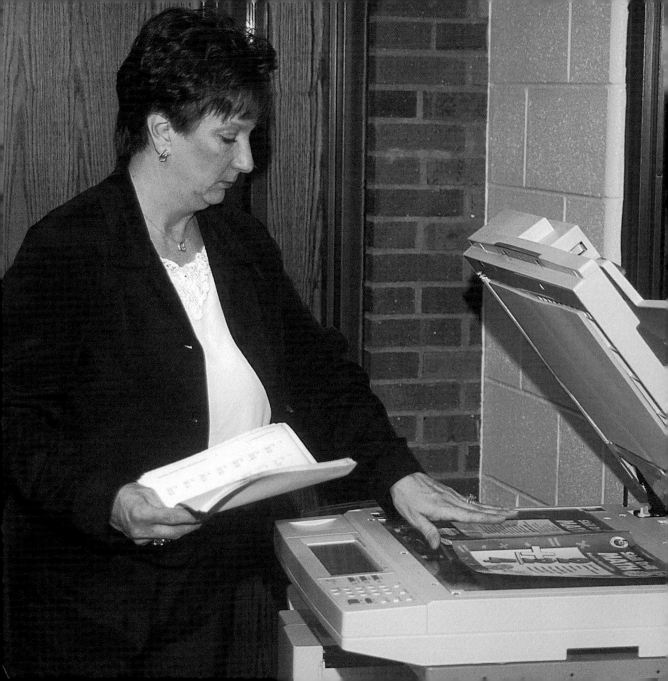

The school secretary is very important to the teachers. She gives them a lot of information on many things. She helps them by typing and copying materials for their classrooms. She also orders their **supplies**.

Making copies for teachers is another part of a secretary's job.

Each day, the school secretary receives mail for the teachers and puts it in their school mailboxes. The school secretary also answers phone calls for the teachers. She takes many messages and gets information for the teachers.

The secretary puts mail and school announcements for teachers in their mailboxes.

Sometimes teachers are gone from school. The school secretary makes sure there is a **substitute teacher**. When the substitute arrives, the school secretary tells the substitute where the classroom is. She makes sure that the substitute has all the information needed to have a good day.

Substitute teachers rely on school secretaries to help them.

In the mornings, the secretary makes announcements over the **intercom system**. She gives the teachers and the students information about the day's events. She also announces important visitors to the school.

Daily announcements give teachers and students important information.

The school secretary is very important to the school principal. The principal relies on the secretary. The secretary types and sends the principal's letters. She prepares many important reports that the principal needs to have. The secretary often has information that the principal needs.

The school secretary is there to help many people. A lot of her jobs are for others. But the secretary has many other responsibilities. Most people do not realize all the things the school secretary does. But most people do know how important she is to the school!

The school secretary works closely with the school principal.

FURTHER INFORMATION

Books

Kalman, Bobbie D. *School from A to Z*. New York: Crabtree
   Publishing Co., 1999.

Roop, Peter, and Connie Roop. *A School Album*. Chicago:
   Heinemann, 1998.

Web Sites
American School Directory

http://www.asd.com/
Locate your own school's web site.

*Being a school secretary is an
   important job!*

GLOSSARY

intercom system (IN ter kom SIS tem) — a loudspeaker used to announce information to everyone in a building

rely on (ree LIE AHN) — depend on

substitute teacher (sub STE toot TEE cher) — a person who fills in for a teacher who is out

supplies (suh PLIZE) — things that are given out when needed

INDEX